A STUDENT'S GUIDE

TO MOVING OUT

A STUDENT'S GUIDE TO MOVING OUT

D.L. SELIN

To order additional copies of this book, contact:
Xlibris Corporation
1-888-795-4274
www.Xlibris.com
Orders@Xlibris.com
34279

CONTENTS

PART 5: SPECIAL RECIPES

INTRODUCTION

A Student's Guide to Moving Out is a pocket size, reference guide. It begins with the practicalities of moving out, such as saving for the initial move, putting together household items, and finding a great neighborhood. Subsequent chapters deal with various aspects involved in living on your own, such as budgeting, paying your bills, and using and managing credit cards.

Because this is a reference guide, you don't have to read it from cover to cover. Just go to the Table of Contents at the front of the book and look up the information that you need. Write in the book. Ample space has been provided in the margins to write notes and record your ideas.

It is my sincerest hope that the information imparted within these pages will help eliminate some of the confusion that comes from not knowing what living on your own is all about. After all, none of us moved out knowing it all!

D.L. Selin

PART 1

SEE THE FUTURE

"One's first book, kiss, home run, is always the best."
—*Clifton Fadiman*

There is a certain magic about firsts: one's first relationship, one's first car, one's first apartment. Your dreams today are tomorrow's history. Time doesn't diminish our memories, if anything, it stamps them forever in our hearts.

In order to make your dreams come true, you have to commit to a course of action. Take that first step; head past that fear so that you can begin to focus on enjoying the journey. Focus on the process, not the outcome. It's all about making decisions. Set your goals high and don't let anyone tell you no. Remember, today is the first day of the rest of your life.

SIMPLE STEPS

~ Formulate a plan.

1. Set your goals—Break your goal into a series of tasks and focus on completing each task.
2. Do some research—what do you need to make it happen?
3. Ask questions
4. Identify possible setbacks—weigh the positives and negatives of your situation before deciding on a course of action.
5. Explore your options and then make an informed decision. There are choices in every situation, even if they are not obvious at first.

Work out your monthly income and expenses before you begin. A budget (Chapter 3) will help insure that important expenses are not overlooked. A budget can serve as your starting point in helping you to track your expenses, control your spending, and increase your savings.

Preparation is the key. The better prepared you are the more likely you are to succeed.

🔖 Do some financial planning.

1. Prepare a monthly budget
2. Start saving

The important things such as your finances, home, and car, should be on a scale small enough that you could easily take care of them yourself.

Just a note!

Man cannot live on bread alone; you will be required to have an income. Your income may be a student loan, financial aid, inheritance, or a job.

You will be required to show proof of income. (Pay Stub, Income Tax Return—W2, T4) Depending upon your age, you may need a co-signer.

"Home is any four walls that enclose the right person."
—Helen Rowland

THERE'S NO PLACE LIKE HOME!

It doesn't matter how carefully we plan, we can still find ourselves choosing routes we never expected to travel, and not all our choices will turn out the way we hope.

Get started by asking yourself these questions:

- How close do you need to live to your place of work or school?
- What amenities are in the area? (i.e., gas station, bank, grocery store)
- How close is the nearest medical center, fire department and police station?
- Is there a bus route, rapid transit system or taxicab company close by?
- Can you walk or ride a bicycle in the area?
- Is the neighborhood safe?
- Are the streetlights working?
- Are there families with children or other young adults living in the area?
- Is there parking on the street or in a secured area?
- Where is the closest Laundromat?

Where do I look?

- The *classified section* in the local newspaper is a good place to look for rental accommodation. There are sections that list apartment and house rentals, room and board situations, and shared accommodations.
- The *yellow pages* in your telephone directory will list Rental Agencies and Property Management Companies.

🔊 A number of free publications list rental accommodations. Look for the blue or green boxes outside grocery and convenience stores.

Check out the neighborhood!

Moving is expensive, you will only want to do it once.

Even if you fall in love with a place at first sight, go back to the neighborhood at different times of the day, and on different days of the week and talk to your potential neighbors. Ask questions about the local area.

Note: File a change of address with your local post office. The post office does not charge for this service, and your mail will be re-directed for 6 months.

3

"We all live under the same sky, but we don't all have the same vision."
—Konrad Adenauer

ROOMMATES

If you are looking for an effective way to minimize the expense of living away from home, sharing an apartment is significantly cheaper than living on your own. Living with a roommate can be a rewarding experience if ground rules and expectations are agreed upon before moving in together. Roommates can be a hassle on occasion but they can also be a plus—you meet all sorts of new people and have someone to share the work of keeping up the apartment.

Make a list of the advantages and disadvantages of living with a roommate.

Things to consider are:

- How responsible is this person?
- How respectful of your privacy and your possessions will this person be?
- How responsible is this person with money?
- How clean is this person?
- What kind of habits does this person have? (smoking, loud music)
- Do you both enjoy the same type of lifestyle?
- Are you looking for a new friend, or just someone to share the rent?

Where do I find a roommate?

The simplest way to find a "safe" roommate is by moving in with someone you already know. If there is no one readily available, you may need to start networking with friends, co-workers, and family. You could run an ad in the local newspaper, make flyers, or put up ads on bulletin boards in your area. There are also a number of on-line roommate services available on the

Internet. You can post a listing as well as review listings in your area. Do use discretion in giving out information about yourself.

The Interview

If your prospective roommate is **NOT** someone you know, suggest meeting for the first time in a public place. Ask the potential roommate to bring along a list of references and a credit report (make sure you do the same).

Your discussion should include:

- What each of you wants in a roommate
- Whether either one of you had a roommate before—was it a positive or negative experience?
- What your occupations are and the hours you work
- If there are any credit problems that may prevent either one of you from co-signing a Lease Agreement
- Pets
- Any medical conditions or problems
- Privacy—common areas and personal space
- Telephone and Computer Usage—paying the phone bill, the amount of telephone and computer time, long distance charges, borrowing the cell phone, etc.
- Friends—how many, how often and how late
- Boyfriends and Girlfriends—staying without paying, eating in, and bathroom time
- Personal Possessions—sharing clothing, makeup, sports equipment, music, etc.
- Playing musical instruments

Clearing up these things in advance will pave the way to having a great roommate relationship. At the end of your interview, if the potential roommate is not suitable, politely tell him/her you don't think it will work out and thank him/her for coming.

If you decide your prospective roommate is the one for you, invite him/her to come and see the apartment.

Finalize Your Living Arrangement

You and your roommate should have a written agreement on how to divide your expenses. This will help avoid financial misunderstandings and make for a more harmonious relationship.

The two of you will be deciding:

- What furniture each of you will be bringing
- Decorating the common spaces
- How the cleaning schedule will be worked out
- Whether the two of you will be buying your own groceries or dividing the food bill in half

Careful planning and good communication skills will ensure that you enter into a friendly agreement and that you remain friends long after the roommate relationship ends.

4

"It's a funny thing about life;
if you accept anything but the best, you very often get it."
—Somerset Maugham

START WITH THE BASICS

When you are starting out, the goal is to get enough furniture to avoid having to live on the floor.

♫ Begin collecting items.

1. Make a Wish List
2. When special occasions arise, encourage your family and friends to purchase gifts for your new home
3. Look through your parents' basement and attic for items they may no longer be using (Donations are graciously accepted)

You will need:

Kitchen table and chairs
Small love seat or sofa
Coffee Table
Lamps—at least two (1 floor lamp and 1 desk lamp)
Shelving—you can be innovative, anything from milk cartons to bricks and lumber (Do not attach them to the walls, they become the landlord's property)
Bed (Box Spring & Mattress)
Dresser

You will also need some of these smaller items:

Vacuum cleaner, broom, and dustpan
Pots and pans
Dishes (they do not have to match)
Cooking bowls
Cutlery
Small kitchen appliances: coffeemaker, toaster, can-opener
Dish rack
Bedding (at least two sets)
Towels (both Bath and Kitchen)
Shower curtain
Toilet Scrubber and Plunger

Collecting items for your home is the fun part of preparing for the move.

PART 2

ONE STEP AT A TIME

1

"We sometimes get all the information, but we refuse to get the message."
—Cullen Hightower

RENTAL/LEASE AGREEMENTS

You have found your dream apartment. The rent is reasonable, the location is perfect, and you are ready to move in. The Agent/Landlord presents you with a Tenancy/Lease Agreement; it appears rather lengthy and the terms are not easy to understand, however, you cannot move in until you sign it.

I cannot stress strongly enough, how important it is to read and understand these documents before you sign them. If you do not understand something in the agreement, ask for an explanation. If you still do not understand what you are signing, ask for help in looking them over. (Perhaps a parent, neighbor, or teacher) Do not sign any document unless you understand what you are signing. These agreements are legal documents and binding by law. Ignorance is not an excuse when it comes to Tenancy/Lease Agreements. You will be held accountable for the terms set out in the agreement should you break it.

The terms outlined below are standard terms found in most Tenancy Agreements.

Tenancy/Lease Agreement—a contract between the Tenant (person renting) and the Landlord (Apartment Owner, Home Owner, Real Estate Service, Rental Agency) outlining the terms and conditions (rules) that you agree to live by while occupying a suite in the building. It may be in writing, it may be orally agreed upon but not in writing, or it may be assumed from the actions of both parties. It is recommended that the contract be in writing. Both Tenant and Landlord are expected to honor the requirements as agreed upon, in the contract.

Offer to Lease—a document stating the cost of the Security Deposit, Pet Fee, (if applicable) Application Fee and the monthly Rent. The document should state the date when the rent is due; if it does not, rent must be paid on the first day of each month.

Term—a designated period
Note: If a tenant terminates the Lease before the term has expired, the tenant will be responsible for the rent until the landlord finds a new tenant.

Possession Date—the date you are legally allowed to move in. If the landlord has not let you move in on the date stated in your Agreement, you will be entitled to a reduction on your rent (they will deduct a portion of the rent for every day that you did not live there). If, for some reason, the landlord has not let you move in within 10 days of the agreed upon date, you will be allowed to terminate the Agreement and get back your rent and Security Deposit.

Renewal Term—upon expiration of your Agreement, you will have the option to either move out or extend the Agreement for another term.

Termination—the end of the Agreement. If your fixed-term Agreement expires and you have not entered into a new Agreement, it is generally acceptable that you may move out without serving a Termination Notice. All rent must be paid up to date, the utilities must be disconnected, and the premises must be clean.

If your Agreement is month by month, you must give the landlord at least sixty days written notice. The Termination Notice must specify the termination date, the rental address and be signed and dated by the tenant.

Inspection Report—a document stating the condition of the suite before you move in. Pay careful attention to this report and fill it out carefully. If anything is stained, broken, missing, or dirty, be sure to write it on the report before you sign, date, and return it. It is a good idea to go over the report with the Landlord before moving in your possessions. This will prevent having to pay for damages that were not caused by you.

Rent—a payment made by the tenant to the landlord for the use of the property. Rent is due and payable on the first day of the month (the amount and term will be stated in your Agreement). Rent may be paid with a check, cash, or money order. If paying in cash, remember to ask for a receipt.

Security Deposit—an amount of money held in trust by the Landlord for the term of your Agreement, to be refunded after vacating the premises providing that the suite be left in the original condition. (The walls and carpets are clean, the appliances are clean and in working condition, the trash has been disposed of, no belongings have been left behind, and there is no damage to the suite.)

Money paid as a Security Deposit is not the rent.

Sublet—to rent the suite to another person when the Agreement is in your name. **This is not allowed without the permission of the landlord!**

Right of Entry—the landlord or his Agent may enter your suite during reasonable daylight hours, to repair, inspect, or show prospective tenants the space. Unless it is an emergency, the Landlord is required to give you notice in writing prior to entering your home.

Default by Resident—the Agreement that you sign is a legal and binding document; thereby holding you responsible for the terms and conditions set out in the Agreement. If you fail to fulfill the obligations agreed upon, the Landlord can sue you. This action will definitely affect your ability to rent another apartment.

There may be a separate page attached to your Agreement called an *Addendum*. The *Addendum* is a list of rules specific to the building you live in. Some of the items covered will address swimming pool rules, noise by-laws, parking rules, laundry room use, rules pertaining to owning a pet, and rules that apply to guests.

2

"The most important trip you may take in
life is meeting people halfway."
—*Henry Boye*

Forming a relationship is a process of building a rapport with people by taking a sincere interest in who they are and what they have to say. Words have the power to build up or tear down a relationship. The key to keeping your relationships on solid ground is to listen to each other and work together to find one area of common ground. In reaching out to others by listening, we help create a foundation of trust and respect, which opens the door to greater understanding, happiness, and peace.

FROM THIS MOMENT ON . . .

- Pay your rent on time
- Obey the rules set out in the Agreement you signed
- Keep the premises in a condition that meet health and cleanliness standards in your area
- Repair any damage caused by you or your guests
- Make sure to get permission for improvements or renovations (this includes painting)
- Purchase Rental Insurance
- Be considerate of your neighbors
- Notify the Landlord immediately if there is a problem involving repairs or service
- Give your termination notice in writing before you vacate the premises

3

"Education is not the filling of a pail, but the lighting of a fire."
—*William Butler Yeats*

RENTER'S INSURANCE

What is Renter's Insurance?

An insurance policy designed to protect you in the event of loss to your personal property due to fire, theft, water damage, vandalism or any number of other incidents. Renter's Insurance also includes liability coverage and loss of use coverage. Renter's Insurance does not cover property damage or injury resulting from natural disasters. (Flood, Forest Fires and Earthquakes)

Why do I need Renter's Insurance?

The owner is required to carry insurance on the building in which you live; however, he is not responsible to you personally for damage to your possessions in the event of a disaster.

How much Insurance will I need?

An insurance broker can help you determine what type of policy to purchase. It is a good idea to shop around for coverage and compare quotes. Insurance policies do not provide unlimited coverage. You may need to purchase a rider, endorsement, or a separate policy to cover expensive items such as artwork, jewelry, computers, and electronic equipment.

Ask your broker about "replacement cost" versus "actual cash value" when determining how your policy will pay out in the event of a mishap.

> ⚡ Make a list of your personal possessions (be sure to include books, CD's, clothing, jewelry, furniture and appliances, electronics, sports equipment)

- Take pictures
- Keep your receipts, manuals and serial numbers together

How much does Renter's Insurance cost?

Prices will vary according to the declared value of your belongings, special coverage needed, and the amount of your deductible. The easiest way to get the lowest price is to take a higher deductible.

PART 3

INVEST IN YOURSELF

"Make the most of yourself for that is all there is of you."
—Ralph Waldo Emerson

MONEY HABITS

The following are guidelines to help you develop ways to manage or change your personal money habits. By setting guidelines, you can learn to live within your means, plan for your future, and eliminate stress caused by an over-abundance of debt.

- 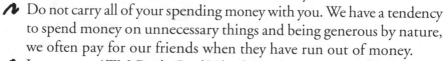 Divide your spending money into weekly amounts. In other words, give yourself an allowance. Start each week with a set amount of money. (If you have prepared a budget, you will know how much your allowance will be.) If you run out of money before the week is out, do not cheat by using a credit card. Go without until the beginning of the next week. You will only do this once or twice before you make sure your allowance will last the full seven days.
- Do not carry all of your spending money with you. We have a tendency to spend money on unnecessary things and being generous by nature, we often pay for our friends when they have run out of money.
- Leave your ATM Bank Card/Check Card at home. Every time you use your card, a small fee will be debited from your account. Those $1.50 charges will add up to twenty or thirty dollars over the course of a month.
- Keep only one credit card. Credit cards are necessary for booking motels, placing deposits and renting cars; however, credit cards carry high interest rates and carrying charges. Credit cards are not a replacement for money. Avoid using your credit card unless you are able to pay the balance within the 30 day billing cycle.
- Use your checking account sparingly. Avoid writing checks for small purchases. Banks charge a small fee for every check that you write.

"A man's fortune must first be changed from within."
—*Chinese Proverb*

BUDGETING

A budget is simply a financial estimate of your monthly expenses. It is a tool used to help you keep track of spending and saving. By using this method, (or one similar to it) you will be able to understand where your money is going. Review and update your budget as your income and expenses change.

For the Month of _____, 20___

	Budgeted Amount	Actual Amount
Income:	_____	_____
Expenses:		
Clothing	_____	_____
Credit Card Exp.	_____	_____
Educational Exp.	_____	_____
Food	_____	_____
Gifts & Entertainment	_____	_____
Insurance	_____	_____
Laundry/Dry Cleaning	_____	_____
Medical & Dental	_____	_____
Rent	_____	_____
Transportation	_____	_____
Utilities	_____	_____
Vehicle Expense	_____	_____

Other: _____   _____

Total: _____   _____

Income - Expenses = Spending Money   _____

3

"A pretty basket does not prevent worries."
—*Congolese proverb*

THE ENVELOPE SYSTEM

Making the budget is easy. Sticking to it is hard.

1. Take 12 envelopes (the number will vary according to your budget) and mark each one with the name of the expense, the payment due date, and the amount due. Staple the bill to the envelope.
2. Divide your expenses between paydays, being careful to note the due date on your bills. You may find that you need to put more money aside from the mid-month paycheck to meet the month-end expenses.
3. Put the required amount into each envelope every payday. Providing that you did not cheat and borrow money from your other envelopes, you should have the cash readily available when your expenses come due.

Note: When paying your bills in cash, get a receipt!

Use the ATM machine sparingly. They carry fees, are tempting to overuse, and make record keeping more difficult. Reconcile your bank account monthly. Keep the debit card slips and compare them against your bank statement.

If your expenses are larger than your income, you may need to re-evaluate your lifestyle and your living arrangements. There are a number of ways to lower your expenses, such as:

- renting a larger place and having roommates
- using the transit system or car-pooling rather than driving
- eating in more often than out

- getting rid of your credit cards
- buying a cellular phone plan that offers free weekend and evening calls, or has rollover minutes
- living within walking distance to your place of work (or school)

4

"The secret of getting ahead is getting started."
—Mark Twain

BANKING

Opening a bank account is the easiest way to establish a credit rating. There are a number of bank accounts available today; the two most common accounts are the Checking Account and the Savings Account.

Checking Account

A Checking Account will allow you accessibility to your funds by using bank issued checks or a check card. Upon opening your Checking Account, you will be required to order personal checks from your Bank.

There is a fee for the purchase of checks; a monthly service fee for the use of the account; and a small fee for every check you write. There is also a fee for using your check card at a branch other than your Member Branch. All fees are automatically debited from your account.

Make sure you understand the banking policies of the branch when you open your account.

Savings Account

Savings Accounts are "interest-earning" accounts. You will earn interest on your money if you leave it in the account. The interest rate will be determined by the bank and paid to your account at pre-determined times. You are allowed to withdraw money from your Savings Account, but the number of withdrawals you may make without penalty may be limited. You will be subject to the same *fee structure* with a Savings Account as you are with a Checking Account.

Banks today offer a full line of personal finance services, from on-line banking to Securities Investment. Choosing the right account helps keep your money moving forward. It's where smart money management begins.

5

"The question shouldn't be,
Will it happen?
But do we want it to happen, and can we help it happen?"
—Peter G. W. Keen

CREDIT CARDS

What is a Credit Card?

A Credit Card is a charge card account with a pre-determined limit offered to the Consumer by a lending institution. "Credit" is a system of allowing customers to pay later for goods and services purchased today. A Credit Card is a form of borrowing money.

How do I get a Credit Card?

The Credit Card Company may send you an application through the mail, internet, or by telephone solicitation. Federal law prohibits Credit Card Companies from sending you a card that you did not request. You must fill out an application form and return it to the issuer. The issuer will check your credit rating prior to approving your credit application.

Credit terms vary among companies. Study your card agreement; it contains important information about annual fees, cash advances, and finance charges.

Terms:

- **Annual Fees**—Credit Card Companies charge an annual membership or participating fee. The fees may range in price from a few dollars to several hundred. This amount is billed to your credit card as a charge once a year.

- **Annual Percentage Rate**—The Annual Percentage Rate is a measure of the cost of credit, expressed as a yearly rate.
- **Billing Cycle**—The time between billing statements—usually 28 to 31 days.
- **Fixed Rate**—An annual percentage rate that does not change throughout the year.
- **Periodic Rate**—The Periodic Rate is a rate applied to your outstanding balance to figure the finance charges for each billing cycle.
- **Transaction Fees**—Some credit card companies charge a fee if you use your card to take a cash advance, make a payment late, or go over your credit limit.

BALANCE COMPUTATION METHODS

You will avoid finance charges by paying the balance of your account in full before the due date.

There are a number of methods used to calculate finance charges.

- **Average Daily Balance**—this method is the most common calculation method. To figure out the balance due each month, the Credit Card Company totals the beginning balance for each day in the billing cycle and subtracts any payments made to your account on the actual date you paid it. The daily balances are added to your billing cycle, the total is then divided by the number of days in the billing period, (usually 30) to arrive at the Average Daily Balance.

Example:

Annual Percentage Rate	*18%*
Monthly Rate	*1 ½% (APR divided by 12)*
Billing Cycle	*30 days*
Previous Balance	*$100.00*
Payment made on the 15th	*$ 50.00*
New Purchase made on the 18th	*$ 50.00*

1. *Take the previous balance of $100.00 and multiply it by 15 days (you made your payment on the 15th) then divide the total by 30 days.*

2. *Take the balance of $50.00 (previous balance minus payment) and multiply that by 3 days (you made a new purchase on the 18th) then divide the total by 30 days.*

3. *Take the new balance of $100.00, (old balance plus new purchase) and multiply that by 12 days, (number of days left in your billing cycle) then divide by 30 days.*

$$\frac{(\$100 \times 15) + (\$50 \times 3) + (\$100 \times 12)}{30 \ days} = \$95.00$$

Take the Daily Balance ($95.00) and multiply that by the monthly rate (1 ½%) to arrive at the finance charge.

$$\$95.00 \times 1 \ ½\% = \$1.43$$

🜚 **Adjusted Balance**—this method will give you until the end of the billing cycle to pay a portion of your balance to avoid interest charges on that amount.

The balance is determined by subtracting your payment received during the current billing cycle, from the previous month's balance at the end of the previous billing period. Purchases made during this billing period are not included.

Example:

Annual Percentage Rate	*18%*
Monthly Rate	*1 ½%*
Balance	*$100.00*
Payments	*$50.00*

1. *Take the balance of $100.00 and subtract the payment of $50.00, leaving a balance of $50.00.*

2. *Multiply the new balance of $50.00 by the monthly interest rate of 1 ½% to arrive at the finance charge.*

$100.00 - $50.00 = $50.00
$50.00 x 1 ½% - $.75

↟ **Previous Balance**—Finance charges are calculated on the amount owing at the end of the previous billing period. Charges and payments made during the current billing cycle are not included.

Using the same information as the above noted example:

The balance is multiplied by the monthly interest rate, to arrive at the finance charge.

$$\$100.00 \times 1 \tfrac{1}{2}\% = \$1.50$$

↟ **Two-Cycle Balance**—the Credit Card Company may use various methods to calculate your balance that make use of the last two months account activity.

Read your agreement carefully. If the Credit Card Company is using this approach, ask what two-cycle method they are using.

You will receive a monthly statement listing your current balance, purchases, payments, and finance charges. Look over your statement carefully. If you find any errors or charges not made by you, notify your Credit Card Company immediately. The Credit Card Company must acknowledge your complaint in writing within 30 days of receiving your written notice. The dispute must be resolved within 90 days.

There is a 24-hour toll-free emergency number printed on the back of your Credit Card. **Write it down.** Notify your Credit Card Company immediately if you have had your card stolen or if you have lost it. Be sure to follow up with a letter to the Credit Card Company stating the date of loss, the account number, and the date you notified them by telephone.

Credit Card Smarts!

↟ If you max out your credit card do not use another one to pay it off
↟ Stay within your credit limit
↟ Pay your balance in full when you receive your statement
↟ Never pay only the minimum payment—pay more

- ↝ Do not use your credit card for cash advances, the interest charges are much higher than for purchases
- ↝ Never take a cash advance to pay your credit card bill
- ↝ Read the fine print on Balance Transfer Checks
- ↝ Hold on to your receipts. Verify the charges on your statement when your bill arrives
- ↝ Draw a line through blank spaces on charge slips to prevent the amount from being changed
- ↝ Keep a record of your account numbers, expiration dates, and telephone numbers of each Credit Card Company

Debt to Income Ratio

How much debt is too much?

When your debt ratio reaches between 25 to 30 percent of your income, your debt ratio is climbing into the danger zone.

To calculate how much debt you have, relative to your current income:

$$\frac{\text{Debt}}{\text{Income}} = \text{debt danger ratio}$$

Let's say your annual income is $30,000. You owe $10,000 on your car and $5,000 on your credit cards. Add your total debt ($15,000) and divide that by your income ($30,000) to arrive at your debt danger ratio.

$$\frac{\$15,000}{\$30,000} = 50\%$$

If your current debt is out of control:

- ☺ consolidate higher interest loans into a loan with a lower interest rate
- ☺ extend your loan repayment periods
- ☺ pay off the higher interest rate loan first

6

"Obstacles are those frightful things you see
when you take your eyes off your goal."
—Henry Ford

CREDIT SCORES AND REPORTS

From the first time you open a bank account, make a major purchase, or apply for a credit card, you begin to establish a Credit Rating. A Credit Rating is a history of your spending habits.

If you have ever applied for a loan, a credit card, a vehicle, or insurance, there is a file called a **Credit Report** about you. This file contains information about where you live, how you pay your bills, if you have ever declared bankruptcy, been sued, or arrested.

This information is used to evaluate your application for things such as employment, credit, lease agreements, and insurance. Having a good Credit Report will make it easier for you to obtain credit and get lower interest rates.

Your **Credit Score** is a point system developed with statistical data to help determine Creditors of your credit worthiness. Your bill paying history, the number of accounts you have, the age of your accounts, and the amount of outstanding debt you are carrying will all play a part in determining your credit score.

According to the Free File Disclosure Rule of the Fair and Accurate Credit and Transactions Act, (in the USA) each of the nationwide consumer reporting companies is required to provide you with a **free copy** of your credit report once a year, if you ask for it.

PROTECTING YOUR CREDIT RATING

- If you are unable to pay your bills on time, contact your creditors and explain to them your situation. Try to work out a modified payment plan that will reduce your payments to a more manageable level. Do not stop paying your bills or ignore your creditors, they may turn your account over to a Collection Agency.

- Once a year ask for a copy of your Credit Report. Go over the report. If there is inaccurate or incomplete information, inform the Reporting Company **in writing** what information is inaccurate. Send copies of supporting documents and a copy of the credit rating to them.

- Consumer Companies must investigate your claims within 30 days of receiving your complaint. When the investigation is complete, the consumer company will furnish you with a report regarding their findings. If they have found in your favor, you may request they send a corrected copy to anyone that requested your report in the last 6 months.

- Don't file for bankruptcy; it stays on your Credit Report for ten years.

- Keep your debt to income ratio under 25 percent.

PART 4

HOME ECONOMICS 101

1

*"Big doesn't necessarily mean better.
Sunflowers aren't always better than violets."*
—Edna Ferber

GROCERY SHOPPING

One of the easiest ways to save money is to become a wise, selective, food shopper.

~ Before you go to the supermarket:

1. Check your pantry to see what you already have
2. Check out the flyers. The best sales are usually on the front and the back
3. Plan your meals ahead of time
4. Do not impulse buy, make a list
5. Clip and use coupons—many coupons offer 2 for 1 products
6. Use rebates and mail in offers
7. Never grocery shop on an empty stomach; we have a tendency to purchase more when we are hungry
8. Go shopping alone

~ At the supermarket

1. Pay with cash. You are less likely to buy what you don't need
2. Look for unadvertised specials
3. Use *store specific* savings cards
4. Buy *family packs* of meat and divide them into single size portions
5. Take advantage of in-season produce. Fresh fruit and vegetables are cheaper than canned or frozen products; they are also healthier for you.

6. Stock up on fresh vegetables and freeze them
7. Avoid pre-packaged, microwaveable and instant food
8. Check the *use by* and *sell by* dates on all products
9. Shop at a *bulk warehouse* for items such as toilet paper, cleaning supplies and dried goods
10. Compare prices on name-brand products and generic brand products. Generic products are the same quality, are usually packed by the same packer, and are less expensive because no advertising costs are built into the price

2

"The choicest pleasures in life lie within the ring of moderation."
—*Martin Tupper*

FURNITURE SHOPPING

Let your curiosity take you on a journey. Visit new places, you may discover treasures you never expected. It's a fact; one person's junk is another person's treasure.

- Attics and Basements—perhaps the best place to start your search. Some of the best pieces of furniture are those *hidden items* that someone put in the attic or basement. Be sure to ask before you reclaim these hidden treasures.
- Garage Sales and Flea Markets—you can find them listed in newspapers, on street corners, in shop windows and on bulletin boards. These are great places to test out your bargaining skills. Flea markets offer the widest variety of merchandise and are the best places to buy china, silver and crystal. For an elegant, informal table setting, choose a theme (or color) and collect individual, orphaned pieces.
- Newspapers—you will find some amazing bargains in the "Used Furniture Section" of the daily paper. In larger newspapers, there may be a section advertising items under $50.00, and often a section giving items away free.
- Secondhand Stores and Thrift Shops—you can find everything from retro clothing and accessories, to household appliances and furniture.
- Hardware Stores—now available at many hardware stores: high quality, wooden, unfinished furniture, requiring assembly and a little paint. This is an inexpensive way to have designer pieces for a low price.
- Department Stores—a great place to look for floor models and discontinued items.

- Furniture Discount Stores—you will find these Warehouse Stores all over the country. They offer a wide variety of furniture and home décor items at reasonable prices.
- Furniture Manufacturers—there are advantages to buying your furniture directly from the manufacturer. You will be able to customize your furniture by choosing from a variety of styles, colors and fabrics. However; the prices will be higher, the order time will be anywhere from four to six weeks, and there will be a delivery charge.
- Retail Furniture Stores—many furniture stores have a *Clearance Room* where you can purchase at below retail price, items that have been discontinued or damaged.

3

"When fate hands you a lemon, make lemonade."
—Dale Carnegie

STAIN REMOVAL GUIDE

✂ Candle Wax—remove excess wax carefully with a dull knife. Place a paper towel over the stain and press with a warm iron. Replace paper towels frequently to absorb the wax. If the wax is on the carpet, use a blow dryer to melt the wax.

✂ Blood—rinse the stain with cold salted water; rub with bar soap, rinse.

✂ Chocolate—soak in warm water using a heavy-duty liquid detergent. If the stain does not come out, try soaking again in a non-chlorine bleach detergent.

✂ Grass—make a paste of granular detergent and water, and rub into stain. Wash in hottest water for fabric.

✂ Gum—apply ice to harden. Scrape with a dull knife. Sponge the back of the stain with a dry cleaning solvent. Rinse. Wash in hottest water safe for fabric.

✂ Ink—saturate the material with an alcohol-based hairspray. Place paper towels under the stain and blot with a rag. Repeat until the stain is gone. Launder as normal.

✂ Red Wine—pour a small amount of white wine or club soda on the stain, it will neutralize the stain as well as absorb the color. Wash in cold water.

✂ Do not mix or combine stain removal products. Work on the stain from the reverse side to prevent it from spreading.

✂ Read the garment labels for washing directions

4

"Life is just a series of trying to make up your mind."
—*Timothy Fuller*

GENERAL RULES FOR TABLE SETTING

Place tablecloth with the center crease in the center of the table; placemats straight, evenly spaced, and even with the edge of the table.

A table centerpiece should be a low arrangement.

A *"cover"* is a complete setting of china, stemware, silver, and linen for one person. The space allowed (per person) should be 50 cm x 60 cm.

1. Place knives to the right of the plates, sharp edges towards the plate. Bread and butter knives placed parallel to the table edge.
2. Place spoons to the right of the knives, bowls up.
3. Place forks to the left of the plate, but if a main course does not require a knife—then place the fork to the right.
4. Silver is arranged in the order in which it will be used, from outside in. Spoons and knives are always grouped separately. Silver should be 3 cm from the table edge.
5. Place glasses at the tip of the knife.
6. Place bread and butter plates to the left of the tip of the fork.
7. Bread and Butter knives are placed across the Bread and Butter plates with the sharp edge toward the center of the plate.
8. Fold napkins in flat squares or oblongs and place to the left of the forks with the open corner to the lower right hand corner. They may also be placed on the dinner plate.
9. There should be a salt and pepper set for every two people.
10. Food is served and removed from the left, using the left hand.
11. Beverages are served and removed from the right, using the right hand.

12. Water glasses are filled three-quarters full just before announcing the meal.
13. When each course is finished, all food service for that course is removed.
14. Remove leftover food first, soiled dishes next, and then salt and pepper shakers.
15. Remove dishes two at a time. Do not stack dishes.
16. Place silver for serving beside the food—not in it.

SOMEONE CARES 1-800 TELEPHONE NUMBERS

Information provided by Child Welfare Information Gateway

United States Better Business Bureau	703-276-0100
Canadian Better Business Bureau	416-766-5144
Association for Children for Enforcement of Support, Inc.	800-738-2237
Alcohol and Drug Abuse Hotline	800-861-1768
American Bar Association	800-285-2221
American Counseling Association	800-347-6647
Child help USA	800-422-4453
Federal Student Aid Information Center	800-433-3243
Grief Inc., American Grief Academy	888-564-6018
The Foundation Center (References for Grant Seekers)	800-424-9836
National Council on Child Abuse and Family Violence	202-429-6695
National Domestic Violence Hotline	800-799-7233
National Center for Victims of Crime	800-394-2255
National Runaway Switchboard	800-786-2929
Parent Effectiveness Training	800-628-1197
Tough Love International	800-333-1069
Rape & Incest National Network	800-656-4673 ext 1
US Department of Health and Human Services	800-368-5779

PART 5

SPECIAL RECIPES

1

*"If I actually ran the world, I'd do it from the kitchen.
That's just how I understand things."*
—Jamaica Kincaid

I've saved the very best for last. Favorite recipes are more than directions for tasty food. They are traditions in the making, a way of sharing. The recipes included in this section are perfect for busy cooks who find little time for cooking. Many require just a few common ingredients and all are simple to make. Experiment with some of the ingredients to give them your own personal touch. Make several on the weekend, freeze them and you'll be ready for the week ahead.

Special thanks to my Chefs Extraordinaire: Christina Barber, Bill Zancocchio, Edna Selin, Beverly Wight, and Elizabeth McAdie, for sharing their recipes with the world.

PLAIN OMELET FOR FOUR

Serves 4

Ingredients:

8   eggs
5   teaspoons butter or margarine
½   cup cold water
1½ teaspoons salt

Directions:

1. In a non-stick frying pan, melt the margarine or butter over moderate heat.
2. In a medium size bowl, add the eggs, water and salt.
3. Beat just enough to blend the mixture.
4. Pour the egg mixture in the pan and reduce the heat to low. As the mixture sets at the edge, lift gently with a knife to let the uncooked mixture flow to the bottom. Continue until the omelet is cooked. Loosen the edges of the omelet. Fold in half and turn out onto plate.

LEMON CHICKEN

Serves 4

Ingredients:

4   bone-in chicken breasts
    Salt
    Fresh ground black pepper
1   lemon, un-peeled, thinly sliced
½   cup melted butter
½   teaspoon thyme

Directions:

1. Heat the oven to 350 degrees.
2. Arrange the chicken pieces, skin side up, in a shallow roasting pan.
3. Sprinkle the chicken pieces with the salt, pepper and thyme.
4. Pour the melted butter over the chicken.
5. Top each piece of chicken with the lemon slices.
6. Bake uncovered for 1 hour.

SWEET AND SOUR MEATLOAF

Serves 4

Ingredients:

1½ pounds of ground beef
1   cup soda cracker crumbs
1   beaten egg
1   Tablespoon garlic powder
½   can tomato soup
¼   teaspoon salt
1   medium onion—chopped up

Sauce:
½   can tomato soup
2   Tablespoons brown sugar
2   Tablespoons prepared mustard
2   Tablespoons vinegar
1   cup water

Directions:

1. Heat the oven to a temperature of 350 degrees.
2. In a medium bowl, combine the ground beef, soda cracker crumbs, garlic powder, salt, onion, egg and soup.
3. Pat into loaf pan. Let sit for about 5 minutes.
4. In a small bowl, combine the remaining tomato soup, brown sugar, mustard, vinegar and water. Pour over the meatloaf.
5. Bake uncovered for 1 ½ hours.

CHILI

Serves 4

Ingredients:

1	lb ground beef
1	large onion—chopped
1	can of chopped tomatoes
1	can of tomato sauce
1	can of red kidney beans
1	can brown beans
2	tablespoons shortening
½	teaspoon vinegar
2	cloves garlic—minced
¼	teaspoon cayenne powder
2	Tablespoons chili powder
	Salt
	Fresh ground pepper

Directions:

1. In a large saucepan, heat 2 tablespoons of shortening over a moderately low heat.
2. Add the ground beef, garlic and onion. Cook, stirring occasionally until the ground beef is brown, about 10 minutes.
3. Pour off excess grease
4. Add the remaining ingredients; bring to a simmer.
5. Reduce the heat to low, simmer uncovered, until thick, about 30 minutes.

LASAGNA

Serves 4

Ingredients:

1½ pounds lean ground beef
1½ teaspoons olive oil
2 cloves garlic, crushed
1 large onion—chopped
1 medium jar spaghetti sauce
1 can tomatoes
1 can mushrooms
½ teaspoon pepper
½ teaspoon oregano
1 package lasagna noodles (about 15 pieces)
1½ teaspoons salt
1 large package mozzarella cheese
1 large package cheddar cheese—shredded

Directions:

1. Heat the oven to 400 degrees. Oil a large baking dish.
2. In a large frying pan, heat the oil over moderately low heat. Add the onion and garlic, cook, stirring occasionally, until starting to soften, about 3 minutes. Stir in the ground beef and cook, breaking it up, until the meat is no longer pink, about 2 minutes. Drain off any excess fat.
3. Add the tomatoes, mushrooms, spaghetti sauce, salt, pepper and oregano and bring to a simmer.
4. In a large pot of boiling, salted water, cook the noodles until just done, about 12 minutes. Drain.
5. In an oven safe baking dish, layer lasagna noodles, sauce, and cheese. Bake until bubbling, about 15 minutes.

BEEF POT ROAST

Serves 4

Ingredients:

	(2 to 3 pound) beef chuck roast
2	Tablespoons cooking oil
¾	cup liquid (may be water, wine or tomato juice)
	Onions, cut into wedges
	Potatoes, medium or tiny
	Carrots
1	Tablespoon Worcestershire Sauce
	Celery, cut into 1" pieces
1	teaspoon Beef Bouillon granules
½	cup cold water
	Salt
	Fresh ground pepper

Directions:

1. Trim the fat from the roast
2. In a large saucepan, heat 2 tablespoons of oil over moderate heat.
3. Add the beef to the pan and brown. Reduce the heat to moderately low.
4. Add the liquid to the pan and cook, stirring to dislodge any brown bits that cling to the bottom of the pan. Stir in the Worcestershire sauce, beef bouillon, salt, and pepper. Bring to a simmer. Cover and continue to simmer, until tender, about 60 minutes.
5. Add the vegetables to the roast and cook (covered) for approximately 1 hour, or until the vegetables are tender.
6. Check often and add small amounts of water as needed.

MEATBALLS AND TOMATO SAUCE

Serves 4

Ingredients:

1 and ¼ pound ground beef
½   cup plain bread crumbs
½   cup Ricotta cheese
1   teaspoon dry parsley flakes
1   teaspoon salt
1   egg
2   Tablespoons olive oil
1   28-ounce can of crushed tomatoes or crushed tomatoes with puree
1   cup water
2   teaspoons basil
1   teaspoon oregano
¼   teaspoon onion salt
¼   teaspoon garlic salt
2   teaspoons salt

Directions:

1. In a medium bowl, combine the breadcrumbs, ricotta cheese, ground beef, one teaspoon salt, and the parsley flakes.
2. Hand mix and roll into uniform size meatballs.
3. In a large frying pan, heat the oil over moderately low heat.
4. Cook meatballs until cooked through and just beginning to brown, about 10 minutes. Remove from the heat.
5. Meanwhile, in a saucepan, combine the crushed tomatoes, water, basil, oregano, salt, garlic and bring to a simmer. Simmer, stirring, about 2 minutes. Add the meatballs and continue cooking on low heat for about 1 hour.

BLACK MIDNIGHT CAKE

Ingredients:

2	cups flour
2	cups sugar
2	teaspoons baking soda
1	teaspoon baking powder
¾	cup cocoa
1	teaspoon salt
1	cup milk
2	eggs
1	teaspoon vanilla
½	cup vegetable oil
1	cup black coffee

Directions:

1. Pre-heat oven to 350 degrees
2. Sift together all dry ingredients
3. Add milk, eggs, vanilla, vegetable oil and black coffee
4. Stir, batter will be very thin
5. Pour into greased baking pan
6. Bake for 35 to 40 minutes

ENGLISH APPLE BETTY

Ingredients:

6   apples—peeled and sliced
     Cinnamon—to taste
½ cup butter
1   cup brown sugar
¾ cup flour
     Ice cream

Directions:

1. Pre-heat oven to 350 degrees
2. Fill a 1 quart casserole dish about 2/3 full with sliced apples
3. Sprinkle with cinnamon
4. Cream butter, sugar and flour together until crumbly
5. Sprinkle over apples
6. Bake for 40 minutes
7. Serve with ice cream

BIBLIOGRAPHY

Other Sources You Might Use:

"Choosing and Using Credit Cards." FTC Facts for Consumers. Online. Internet. January 1999. Available *http://www.ftc.gov*

"Finances." Visa Student. Online. Internet. 3 October 2001. Available *http://www.rankit.com/finances/*

Ministry of Housing, Recreation and Consumer Services, "Tenant and Landlord Rights and Responsibilities," *B.C. Consumer Education Series,* (January, 1994)

"Renters Info." Online. Internet. 14 September 1999. Available *http://www.rent.net/rentersinfo/*

Quotes:
MMII IMP AB. *"Recipes for the Soul"*